FORGIVE

Of Course You Can!

By: Angela Bowden

Forgive Of Course You Can

Forgive Of Course You Can

Copyright © 2020 Angela Bowden

All rights reserved. No portion of this book may be reproduced, stored in a retrieval system, or transmitted in any form or by any means; electronic, mechanical, photocopy, recording, scanning, or other, except for brief quotations in critical reviews or articles, without the prior written permission of the author.

Cover design by Kelly Teno at Truce Creative.

Literary consulting, developmental editing, and formatting, by Clara Rose at Intentional Influence.

Published by RoseDale Publishing
3030 Starkey Blvd, Suite 207
Trinity, Florida 34655

ISBN: 978-0-9975120-9-0

Forgive Of Course You Can

Dedication

This book is dedicated to my children, Javaris, Shante, and Eboni, and to my grandchildren, David and Javaris Jr. (Jay). You have made me stronger, better, and more fulfilled than I could have ever imagined.

Believe it or not, our disagreements were instrumental in showing me the importance of forgiving and moving on. Yes, you too have ministered to me, both in love and forgiveness.

I love you with all that I have.

Forgive Of Course You Can

Contents

Dedication 5

Acknowledgments 9

Preface 11

Meet My Family 17

Hurt and Alone 29

Repeat Offender 43

Innocent Bystanders 55

Mind Body and Soul 67

The Elephants 79

Forgive and Be Free 91

Transformation 103

The Awakening 115

Triumphant 127

About the Author 135

Bibliography 137

Forgive Of Course You Can

Acknowledgments

I'm eternally grateful to God for placing this book on my heart; I thank Him for walking and talking with me through every chapter.

To God be All the Glory!

Forgive Of Course You Can

Preface

I wrote this book for those of you who have given up (or feel like giving up) on finding that place in your heart to forgive.

If this book is in your hands right now, that's an indication to me that you have not given up. It means the desire to forgive, to let go, and move on, is still resting in your spirit.

I get it, there was a time in my life when I was exactly where you are. I longed to be happy and free, and I want you to be free too.

Sharing my story, my journey to forgiveness, was placed on my heart many years ago, but I put it off. I didn't feel like I had enough to say. I didn't think my story was enough or could reach other hurting people, until I began to look back over my life and see where the Lord brought me from, and how he carried me through. That's when my heart poured out onto these pages.

I'm so happy you're here. I have already prayed my journey shared in this book, would inspire hope and help bring you to a place of healing, which will ultimately bring you closer to the Father.

I have included *Reflection Questions* at the end of each chapter. Sometimes it's good to ponder certain things and jot them down. It might be helpful in sorting out your thoughts.

Remember, you can do all things through Christ who strengthens you!

Forgive Of Course You Can

Forgive Of Course You Can

"The seed of Unforgiveness can go un-detected; be careful to guard your heart." - Angela Bowden

Forgive Of Course You Can

Chapter 1

Meet My Family

My name is Angela, I am 59 years old, a divorcee, and a mother to three adults. As a Christian, I struggled with unforgiveness for many years.

Let me start by saying family, my family, means everything to me.

Before I share my journey to forgiveness, I need to introduce you to the dynamics of my family. There is my mom, my dad, and eight children. I'm in the middle of the mix with four older siblings and three younger ones. (Sadly, we lost our eldest brother to cancer some years ago.) Growing up, needless-to-say, it was a very busy house.

Mom was a housewife but also the disciplinarian - and she didn't play. My dad was the provider and over-seer of everything else; he was an insurance salesman.

Every year the company my dad worked for would have their summer party on the beach. I miss those days; it was always so much fun - beach bonfires and seafood.

Growing up my dad would often bring home ABC pizza. To this very day, ABC pizza is my favorite pizza, in the whole wide world.

We grew up in a Christian home, a strict Christian home I might add. However, as tight as it was, we didn't miss out on too much. My mom and dad made sure we had as much as was necessary to keep us entertained and busy in our own back yard. It was nice, I have plenty of childhood memories with my brothers and sissies.

The boys had minibikes to ride around on, and the girls had tea sets and easy bake ovens. My brothers had the mechanical boxing men and liked to build miniature race cars. We had a pool and a croquet game; we had all the good toys, and we even had a play and tell.

Occasionally, we would pretend to have a party and cut up snickers bars and divide Cheetos on our plates for dinner, but my absolute best memories are from when we would play church!

Church was a regular part of our lives; we knew just how to recreate it at home. We would preach and shout... it was sooo much fun. With a broomstick and mop as guitars, and a spatula for a microphone, we played that old tambourine and sang our hearts out.

We would listen to Aretha Franklin's gospel album. *How I Got Over* was one of our favorite songs, it was up-beat so we could shout and dance to that one. The best church song was *Jesus Will Fix It*, by the Williams Brothers. It was a long song, so everyone got a part to sing.

We could be in the family room all day singing and shouting, mom never stopped us or came in to quiet us down. I think she liked hearing us play church. Little did she know, when she wasn't home, we would sneak and turn on the blues… we call it R&B now. Those were indeed the good ole days. Like I said, we were NEVER bored.

Mom didn't particularly like us going to other people's houses, but she would sometimes break down and allow us to go home with a friend from church. More often, she would allow them to come to our house. Of course, our preference was to go to their house, they had more freedom than we did, and their parents were much more lenient. They were even allowed to wear shorts! Yep, they did a lot of things we would never think about doing, and it was fun.

Like most brothers and sisters, we fought, well I did. I physically fought with all my brothers and sisters. Funny though, they never fought with each other. I was always the one they had to calm down. Not that I had a temper, I just believed in standing my ground. I guess I was a little rebellious, I was the one to sass my dad out loud and my mom under my breath.

My mind goes back to a time I humiliated my dad in front of company. For as long as I live, I don't think I will ever forget it. I sassed my dad in front of one of his friends. I remember him gritting his teeth, to ground his anger, but he was able to summon my mom to get me.

I am not proud of that moment and to this very day I wish I could take it back. It was one of the most disrespectful, dishonorable things I had ever done to him. He was then and has always been, everything to us, and he did not deserve that.

It's been over forty years since that day, but it still comes to mind occasionally. Every time I think about it, I want to tell him again (just in case he forgets) how sorry I am for hurting him. My heart is truly sorry.

My dad would usually leave the corporal punishment to mom, however, every now and then dad would pop us for something. Mom, she knocked us all the way down, if she thought we were talking back, even if it was under our breath!

My older brother and I fought the most, he was stubborn and so was I. He turned the TV off, I'd turn it on, he'd turn it off again and I'd turn it back on… until we made a mistake and touched each other, that's when the fighting started.

I never won, my brothers have always been muscular guys, but that did not stop me. I know they hated to deal with me that way, but when I got mad, it was on. After the fight, we always moved on. I don't remember being angry after the fights, we just continued being brothers and sisters until the next fight, or should I say "my" next fight.

Mom loved her kids and she was very protective of us. She never allowed us to spend the night at someone else's house. She felt every child should be under their own roof at night. She would say, "I only know what we do here, I have no idea how anybody else runs their house. I need to know you are safe and if you're in this house, I'm gonna make sure you're safe."

As strict as home was, we didn't lack anything, and there was definitely enough of us around to entertain each other. As a child our house was home, and we loved it.

Growing up, I loved my mom, I thought she was the most perfect person in the world. When I became an adult and moved out, I still talked to my mom every day. I would marvel at my friends who lived in a different city than their mom. I could never see myself living more than 30 minutes from her, she was too important to me. I'd even tell the guys I dated, the only problem we would have is if they asked me to leave Tampa and my mom.

I remember the times I would brag about my mom to others, how she did not curse and did not drink. For me she was the epitome of a woman of God, and she really was. She still loves the Lord and I still love her - very much.

As the years went by, somewhere, somehow, things begin to change, little by little the queen of my heart, my mom, grew distant to me. As the years of my life played out, I found myself caught up in the grips of unforgiveness.

This is my story… this is my journey.

Are you able to pinpoint where your struggle with unforgiveness began?

Forgive Of Course You Can

Forgive Of Course You Can

Forgive Of Course You Can

"Unforgiveness is a self-made prison. However, the key to freedom is in your hands." – Angela Bowden

Forgive Of Course You Can

Chapter 2

Hurt and Alone

I guess by now you have concluded that my journey to forgiveness, my story, starts with my mother. To tell you the truth, I'm not sure exactly when or how it all started. Even now as I'm writing, I try and go back in my mind to find a starting point, only to realize there were quite a few situations where I was offended, and left feeling hurt and alone.

As an adult, there were so many times I felt like the black sheep of the family. In my eyes, everyone was loved and being loved except for me. I kept trying to figure out what I had done that was so bad, that my mom would treat me so differently from my other siblings... I mean, I know she loved me, but it didn't feel like love.

I had never experienced these feelings as a child growing up, never felt unloved, cutoff, there was nothing but love at home.

We're all adults now, how did I go from a wonderful childhood experience and being a doting daughter, to feeling like a motherless child? Needless-to-say, this was a very hard place for me. I felt like I couldn't talk to anyone about how I was feeling, after all this was MOM. I shared her with my other brothers and sisters, who seemed to be okay. How could I talk to them and have them understand where I was coming from? Would they even believe what I was experiencing in my relationship with mom?

How in the world was this happening to ME? Talk about feelings of isolation, cut off, distant, abandoned... I experienced these feelings to the worst degree. I didn't feel safe or comfortable telling anyone, so I kept it all to myself. It churned and churned and churned, until it developed into a bitter root of unforgiveness.

I felt so cut-off from my mom that I prayed for a mother figure. By now I was a divorced mother of 3, with a lot of issues and I needed a mother to turn to. There was a lot going on in my life; a failed marriage, I had lost my house to a fire, my kids were acting out, and I was trying to make ends meet for my family. I felt like I was on an ocean, in a dingy, with no land in sight. Many times, I needed a shoulder to cry on, which should have been my mom's shoulder, right!?! But I felt like I had no mom, not one I could talk to anyway. I was emotionally disconnected.

The Lord answered my prayers for a mother figure... her name was Regina. I met Ms. Regina through her daughter, who was a good friend of mine. She lived in California but we kind of kept in touch after we met. Ms. Regina was a seasoned Christian lady with a lot of wisdom. The more we talked, the more I was able to confide in her about what I was going through. Ms. Regina was my stand in mom, proof once again, God can and will fill every void in our life.

I've often thought about how Ms. Regina and I met - it was the right time. I had no idea she would be the shoulder for me to cry on, someone that I trusted would listen to me and hear my heart, without judging me or blaming me. Ms. Regina was a true prayer warrior.

As I journeyed through this dark, lonely place in my life, I realized that to some degree, victims of abuse deal with the same kind of fear, not the scary monster fear, but fear of being rejected and not believed. So, you just keep it to yourself, deal with it, and live with it. I had never understood why abuse victims would say they were fearful or afraid to tell anyone about their abuse. It was for fear of not being believed, I get it now! Especially if it's a relative; your mother, father, sister, brother, aunt, or uncle. These people are supposed to love and protect us from abusers, not be the abuser. So, you just shut down as it eats away at your life e-v-e-r-y day.

Later in life I realized I had done the same thing. I had slipped into a self-protect or self-preservation mode. You just kind of give up on looking for someone to help ease the pain or make some sense out of it.

I remember early on, talking to my younger sister about what was going on, because she was (I believed) the only one who knew firsthand what I was dealing with and the pain it caused me.

However, as time went on, I could see how it was taking a toll on her and how painful it was for her to process. Eventually I stopped talking to her about it, the last thing I wanted was for my sister to be burdened with my issues.

It's funny how you can have such a big, happy family; hang out, and have fun, but at the same time have this gnawing ache inside of you. As close as I was with my brothers and sisters, I still felt so alone.

I recall the time my sister wanted to help purchase food for me and the kids, while my mom and dad were out of town. Well, mom found out and decided her help would be more beneficial for the trip she was about to take, with my other siblings (who were employed), and would not allow my sister to help me. That really hurt me - it was food stamps - not money.

Sometimes when Mom prepared dinner, she would cook extra food for me and the kids to eat... so she knew I was struggling. Needless-to-say, my sister was flabbergasted when mom told her they could use the help for the trip.

Of course, my sister tried to push back, but mom always had her way - and nobody really stood up to her, they just let mom be mom. I can hear my sister saying, over and over, "I don't understand." It was times like these, that began to take a toll on my sister, I could tell.

My mother is one of the reasons the relationship between me and my son is strained to this very day. The things she said about me, to my own son. Of course, today is a new day and he's a grown man now, able to make his own decisions.

Now this may sound a little crazy. Some years ago, when I lost a close friend of mine, as I was telling my mom about it, I started to cry. She hugged me, but as she embraced me, through my grief I was thinking, "Wow, I feel nothing." The thing is, she may have truly been sympathetic, but by now, scar tissue had developed and I only associated pain with my Mom.

You see, I was so deep into unforgiveness, I could not associate love with anything my Mom did. I never felt like my Mom didn't love me, I'm her daughter, how could she not. Again, it just didn't feel like love.

I could go on and on about me and my mom, and the challenges we faced in our relationship. I lived through the pain of it for many years. However, my point is not to detail everything that happened between us, or to make my mom look like a monster. My intent is to give you a glimpse into just how deep I was buried in the grave of unforgiveness and how I got there.

As the relationship with my mom continued to spiral down, I began to wonder why and how this had happened. Why me, what did I do? Every negative emotion you can imagine was creeping in; anger, bitterness, holding a grudge, sadness... how could I ever let go of these feelings, these thoughts?

How do you unthink something? How do you not feel an offense? How do you start anew? How do you forget about the wrong deed or word, when it hurt so bad?

How do you get to the place where you walk away? When do you stop crying and stop trying to make sense of it? When do you stop asking WHY, knowing no one is going to answer you back?

We've all heard that unforgiveness hurts you not

them and that's why we should forgive. Well yeah, all that sounds good in theory, but in practice it can feel impossible.

As a matter of fact, we may have even said it out loud, "I will never forgive him/them/her for that," and you really believe that you can't. Guess what, you can! Trust me, I know it can be very painful to forgive, but I also know it's even more painful to NOT forgive... it pollutes your soul.

Nothing I tried at the time worked for me, I didn't realize that my heart was not ready yet. As a matter of fact, at the time I didn't even know that my heart had anything to do with unforgiveness. I later came to realize it was a heart issue.

I began to turn to scriptures for hope.

Matthew 11:28-30

28 "Come to me, all you who are weary and burdened, and I will give you rest.

29 Take my yoke upon you and learn from me, for I am gentle and humble in heart, and you will find rest for your souls.

30 For my yoke is easy and my burden is light."

Forgive Of Course You Can

What emotions were stirred up when reading this chapter, and how did you handle it?

Forgive Of Course You Can

Forgive Of Course You Can

Forgive Of Course You Can

"Warriors are built to weather many storms; Warrior." – Angela Bowden

Forgive Of Course You Can

Chapter 3

Repeat Offender

So, what do you do, when you think you have healed, or that the healing process has finally begun, and then bam... you end up picking yourself up off the ground? A word or deed from the offender has once again pummeled you to the ground. I say pummeled because words, as many of you may know, can cut like a knife; the sting of words can be comparable to a physical blow.

What in the world can you do when you are dealing with repetitive offenses from the same person? Forgiveness might be easier if the offense was an isolated incident, but when the same person repeats the offence over and over, it's just hard.

How do you have a meaningful relationship with someone, anyone for that matter, that continues to hurt you, that doesn't think he or she has done anything wrong? How do you open your heart again to that person?

For me there were times when things seemed to be okay with my mom. Times when I felt like I had finally moved on and was able to let bygones be bygones. But there was always another blow lurking around the corner that would push me back to square one and push me deeper into that dark pit. It was very painful, heartbreaking, confusing, and extremely frustrating. The turmoil you experience on the inside is constantly being fueled by yet another painful incident.

At the end of the day, all I really wanted was some sort of acknowledgement. She had hurt me and even if it wasn't intentional, she had still hurt me. But instead of validation for my feelings, another blow came, sometimes even more hurtful than the one before.

I found myself wanting my mom to feel the pain she was inflicting. Beware, this kind of wrong thinking gets you in trouble!

These thoughts can be just as destructive as unforgiveness. As a Christian, this was wrong thinking and another opportunity for the enemy to take advantage of me. But I wanted her to somehow pay for what she was doing to me.

Of course, I didn't want anything bad to happen to my mom, I was just hoping maybe, something would trigger her to call me. I longed to hear her say, "You know what, I'm soooo sorry for any pain I've caused, I'm so sorry if I hurt your feelings, I'm so sorry if I hurt you."

Unfortunately for me, that day never came. As a matter of fact, mom seemed to not have a care in the world. At least that was what it looked like to me; from my point of view. Of course, my perspective was a bit skewed by the hurt that was blurring my vision. Sometimes when we're going through difficulties in our lives, it appears that everyone is happy but you!

Let me tell you something, forgiving someone that continues to offend you is a very hard thing to do - but I'm a living witness it is possible... you can do it.

I can't even begin to tell you how many times my mom has hurt me by something she has said or done. A few times I tried talking to mom about something she said or did. She would just spin it on me; saying I took what she said the wrong way or say that my feelings are too easily hurt. She even blamed me for what transpired, she never accepted responsibility for anything.

Mom never seemed to show remorse, I guess because she didn't feel like she had done anything wrong. Even if I was *too sensitive*, my mom never owned any part of what happened or the ache in my heart.

But you know what, we are all human. Our parents and other loved ones will fail us at times, they'll disappoint us and betray us. However, none of these offenses are unforgiveable, painful – yes… but no matter what, healing is available through forgiveness.

I'm sure you've heard people say, and maybe you have even made the same comment, that certain things are unforgiveable, but that's simply not true.

For years I did not see or even acknowledge unforgiveness as a sin, which I've come to realize was part of my problem. Forgiveness is a commandment from God, at some point you must get to a place where you stop hoping God will show *them their sin* and allow God to show *you your own sin*.

There are consequences to all sin, nobody gets away with anything, but that's God's business not mine! The Lord reminds us in His word that we all fall short of perfection (Romans 3:23 - NIV)

Think about it, though we may not be perpetrating an offense specific towards someone, we all sin. Are you a liar, do you gossip, are you an adulterer, or do you have a hateful heart? The list goes on and on. What other things might we be guilty of, yet we continue to go to God and ask for his forgiveness? Hmm, I guess, if we look at it that way, we all are repeat offenders.

Matthew 18:21-22

21 Then Peter came to Jesus and asked, "Lord, how many times shall I forgive my brother or sister who sins against me? Up to seven times?"

22 Jesus answered, "I tell you, not seven, but seventy-seven times."

Forgive Of Course You Can

Was there a time when you thought you had healed, only to feel the sting again?

Forgive Of Course You Can

Forgive Of Course You Can

Forgive Of Course You Can

"Don't let the shrapnel of unforgiveness injure the innocent."
– Angela Bowden

Forgive Of Course You Can

Chapter 4

Innocent Bystanders

I remember a conversation I once had with a friend, I don't recall what it was about, but I do remember something she said that shocked and hurt me. "You're always down about something… are you ever happy?"

Her candid observation hit me like a ton of bricks. It felt like a gut punch, in part because she was some years younger than me and was trying to nurture me toward emotional health. It was a bit embarrassing, after all I was her older friend and should have been an example for her. Mostly there was a realization that I had become a Debbie Downer!

The unforgiveness I was harboring was morphing me into someone I did not know and was even strange to my friends. I had to really think about that. Who wants to be around someone who's always complaining or always walking around with a hung down head? I knew I didn't, but somehow, I had become that person.

I had once been the life of the party, the bubbly one. I had been the one that could see or bring sunshine to any situation... but not anymore. The joy I once had was overpowered by resentment, anger, and bitterness.

My relationships with my friends had begun to suffer. I was hypersensitive, so I would lash out at my friends and other family members, sometimes making accusations that had no merit whatsoever. Not only were my relationships with family and friends taking a hit, but my relationship with the Lord was also being challenged... this thing was serious!

I found myself having an attitude with people for no reason... seriously, NO reason. Over time I developed trust issues because when you're actively dealing with a broken heart you *side eye* everybody. Everyone looks like or has the potential to be a perpetrator. Looking back, I was angry with anyone that appeared to be happy. After all, they were supposed to be the people that loved me, for real. They were supposed to step in and rescue me from my unspoken misery, not move on through life without me.

I never stopped to consider the truth. How would they know I was going through hell and felt so alone? How would they know anything, since I never told them? They didn't know, they just thought I was acting funny, so they gave me my space. But I did not want space, I needed someone to talk to... someone should have known that, right? In my pain I was irrational. I kept it to myself but expected that someone should have seen something was wrong. I was so mad at anyone who ignored me, and I blamed innocent people for my state of mind.

Everybody became a target, and everyone was on my hit list. I lashed out at people I loved, and they were clueless as to why. Then they would wonder what they had done wrong, trying to figure out what had set me off. Little did they know, the root cause had happened weeks, months, or years before.

Those poor innocent people had no idea they were just casualties of war, innocent bystanders that got caught in the shrapnel of my pain. It wasn't fair... I knew they were being blindsided by my pain, but they didn't know.

One might think, as I slowly began to realize what was happening, I would get a grip on my ugliness and make a conscious decision to pay attention to my words and my attitude. Nope... nothing changed. It just fueled the flame that was already ignited inside of me.

Unforgiveness is very heavy and it was wearing me out. When you're operating in that kind of spirit, you're just so sensitive. It's like having an open sore, everything hurts it. If anybody gets too close, you start shielding yourself from the potential pain. Your mind starts to think about things, re-hashing everything ever said or done to you. You're so open, you're so sensitive, and the enemy of your soul just continues to pour more and more bad memories into your open sore. You've probably heard the saying, *hurting people hurt people…* it's true.

That open sore becomes a container to hold the many offenses. You might find yourself thinking back to elementary school, when your first-grade teacher made you so mad or back six years ago when the cash register lady was rude to you. Anything negative, that has ever happened to you, starts to brew all over again. You are saving all those things in your container of unforgiveness. Why? Because your container is open, you never cut off or capped off that seed of unforgiveness and it continues to grow.

That ugly thing affected my relationships with people who had absolutely nothing to do with what I was going through. More importantly it affected my relationship with God; my worship, my prayers, and my praise, everything was taking a hit. The last thing I needed to do in-the-midst of my pain was isolate myself from God, but I found myself drifting. Thank God, He knew where I was, and He understood. I didn't know it at the time and sometimes I felt like he wasn't on my side either. That's when things started to get really scary.

I think, when I found myself wondering why God had not stepped in and why God had not made good on His promises *to never leave me nor forsake me*, that's when I knew I was really in trouble.

Even then I could not turn things around. I was still taking on fire. I was still being offended and getting angrier and more bitter. Something had to change but I did not know what else to do. I felt like just giving up and not trying to fight the feelings anymore. I convinced myself, if I could just get through it, then it would eventually go away, but that didn't work either.

I didn't know it at the time… however, slowly but surely the Lord began to show me what happens when you operate with an un-repented heart. Yes, I needed to repent. I didn't realize I was doing anything wrong… after all, I felt I was the victim, the offense was against me. I'm supposed to be a little salty, right?

Well, apparently the bible says something different.

The word of God warns us about being quick to

point out the speck in someone else's eye but dismissing the speck in our own eye. (Matthew 7:3)

It doesn't say *unless the other person is at fault…* there were no clauses included in that verse giving us permission to judge others. We must always examine ourselves, always examine our hearts, lest we fall into the same snare. I needed to repent for all my sinful thoughts and feelings, because I was offensive. I had become the thing I was trying to escape.

Psalm 34:18

The Lord is close to the brokenhearted and saves those who are crushed in spirit.

Did you notice a change in your interactions or relationships with others during those times?

Forgive Of Course You Can

Forgive Of Course You Can

Forgive Of Course You Can

Forgive Of Course You Can

"Honor and protect You. Nurture You - all of You." – Angela Bowden

Forgive Of Course You Can

Chapter 5

Mind Body and Soul

We know that Cancer, if left untreated, will contaminate every cell, tissue, and organ in your body. If not dealt with, it will eventually kill you. Unforgiveness does the same thing, when left untreated. It will literally make you sick spiritually, physically, and emotionally.

I dealt with unforgiveness for so long, there were days I felt like I was carrying actual weights (dumbbells) on my body. I can recall times that I was so weighed down, it felt like I was literally pulling my own body. The heaviness is crazy! No one wants to live day-in and day-out like this... emotional and mental suffering is exhausting.

The horrible effects of unforgiveness opens the door to a myriad of feelings and emotions, it affects you mentally, physically, and spiritually, in no specific order. It robs you of your energy. You're in a spiritual battle, it's a fight every day to just maintain or regain a sense of peace in your life.

You become sleep deprived, because at the end of the day, when things get quiet, your mind starts to replay the day and guess what pops up first?

You guessed it, the offense. Your mind replays the event until you finally fall asleep... which hardly ever comes easy.

Unforgiveness is depressing and oppressing. Depending on how you handle pressure or stress, you might start to gain or lose weight, to compensate for the state of mind you are in.

The Rev. Yvonne D. McCoy, M.Div., Retired Chaplain from Norton Women's and Children's Hospital, published this article on the matter.

She said, *"The word "forgive" means to wipe the slate clean, to pardon, or to cancel a debt."*

In her experience, generally, we avoid forgiveness for two reasons: we don't want to let the person off the hook, and we think we are shielding ourselves from being hurt again by holding on to the pain, because the pain reminds us of how devastating the offense was.

Be assured, no one is getting away with anything, the offender's actions have consequences, but only they can own them. They can't run, and they can't hide from an all knowing and all-seeing God.

Likewise, there are also consequences for the offended one, when we choose to hold on to the offense. *Remember, sin is sin is sin* - there are no exceptions to the rule. You don't get a lighter sentence because you are the offended. Let me break it down this way - you're going to get in just as much trouble as the offender, for holding on to the offense. Unforgiveness is SIN - period.

Reverend McCoy shared, *"Evidence-based research suggests that feelings of anger, hurt, and emotional pain release toxic chemicals inside our bodies, that damage organs and our ability to think creatively. This contributes to a variety of diseases, including heart attacks, cancer, ulcers, migraines, and high blood pressure."*

In-light-of these terrible outcomes, forgiveness is one of the most important steps a person must take on the path to healing. On the other hand, the emotions of love, peace, patience, and kindness produce a physical response that releases endorphins, which heal the body.

"Forgiveness takes an act of the will that sometimes does not come easily. It is intentional and voluntary. The victim person must actively and willingly commit to a change of feelings and attitudes in regard to the offense. Forgiveness is a way of letting go of the negative energy around the incident."

When you are free from the crippling power of unforgiveness, you will gain energy, breathe easier, and receive mental, physical, spiritual, and emotional healing. It is important to remember that forgiveness is not granted because a person deserves to be forgiven. Instead, it is an act of love, mercy, and grace that brings healing to the giver and to the offender.

Holistic practitioner Sheryl Walters published an interesting article in Natural News about the topic of forgiveness, she said the following.

> Dr. Frederic Luskin of Stanford University is studying how forgiveness can help people become healthy. The 150 volunteers who have taken part in the Stanford Forgiveness Project say that letting go of the hurt caused by other people or by forces, they see as being outside themselves, is not just one of the greatest emotional releases; they feel better physically, as well.
>
> *"Getting angry and needing to forgive are universal phenomena, but the skills to forgive are inadequately taught."*
>
> Holding on to anger for too long can obviously affect a person's emotional health. But hanging on to that anger, Dr. Luskin says, can also seriously affect people's physical health.
>
> Physically the body is in a state of stress.

Muscles tighten, causing imbalances or pain in the neck, back, and limbs. Blood flow to the joints is restricted, making it more difficult for the blood to remove wastes from the tissues and reducing the supply of oxygen and nutrients to the cells. Normal processes of repair and recovery from injury or arthritis are impaired. Clenching of the jaws contributes to problems with teeth and jaw joints. Headaches can become a problem. Chronic pain may get worse.

Blood flow to the heart is constricted. Digestion is impaired. Breathing may become more difficult. Anger can seriously impair the immune system, increasing the risk of infections and illness.

Luskin cites several studies that show how anger can affect the cardiovascular system by adding to a person's general level of stress. Other studies have indicated that patients who have had heart attacks have been able to improve their physical health by practicing forgiveness and working to feel more tolerant and less angry.

Additionally, Dr. Luskin says, When the body releases certain enzymes during anger and stress, cholesterol and blood pressure levels go up, not a good long-term position to put the body in. Forgiveness has been shown to lower blood pressure naturally. The bottom line, we can eat healthy and take care of ourselves on a physical level, but if our hearts are filled with anger, our bodies are not in optimum health.

Isn't it interesting, that God himself also tells us to live in a way that is good for us spiritually but ALSO good for our bodies!

Proverbs 17:22

22 A cheerful heart is good medicine, but a crushed spirit dries up the bones.

Have you noticed any physical changes that can be attributed to unforgiveness?

Forgive Of Course You Can

Forgive Of Course You Can

Forgive Of Course You Can

"Nothing is more powerful than your will." – Angela Bowden

Forgive Of Course You Can

Chapter 6

The Elephants

I imagine everyone has been to a circus, or some other animal exhibit, where elephants are in a simulated, natural habitat. Or as natural as it can be while they're caged or chained... I'm just saying. We see this giant, humongous, creature shackled to a stake in the ground, or some other object designed to detain them. The trainers seem to move around the elephants with no regard for their size and obvious power.

When looking at them I often wondered why the elephants didn't break free... you know, just pull up the stake and walk away. Perhaps they might get some sort of electrical charge sent through their bodies if the stake sensed a struggle. It was the only thing that made sense to me, but it was just a theory. Here is what I NOW know about these elephants.

When these elephants are calves, at a very young age, they are chained or shackled to a stake in the ground. They tug and pull at the restraint, but they are not strong enough to break free, and eventually they stop trying. As they grow, they continue to be chained to the stake. Over time, they become an adult elephant that has been conditioned to believe they have a very limited range, so they spend their lives moving within the confines of their tether.

Even though it's no longer necessary, the trainers keep them tethered to the stake. The elephant must continue to believe he is restrained, or the trainers will lose the ability to control him. If the elephant discovers how powerful he is, he can no longer be bound by a stake… or anything else for that matter.

The captive elephant has no idea how much power he possesses. He is the largest, most powerful creature walking the face of the earth, yet he has no idea that one tug of his leg can set him free.

Little does the elephant know, everything he needs to set himself free has been made available to him through creation. Unfortunately, his mind has been conditioned to believe he cannot be free, that he cannot move about, and he cannot walk unless someone moves him.

Realistically, the trainer's work is done, they don't need to do anything else to secure the elephant. They've been successful in brainwashing the elephant... this mammoth being, is now chained, tethered, and shackled to a memory.

As I studied the plight of the elephants, I thought about how conditioned our minds have become when it comes to forgiving. Like the elephants, the offense may have happened years and years ago, maybe even when we were a child, but the memory of the offense continues to haunt and keep us chained, tethered, and shackled to that ugly place, that memorial in our mind.

My friend, the offense is now a memory, it really is. You're not there anymore, it's in your past. Even if it happened last week, today is a new day... yesterday is a memory. You must begin to focus on your future and the love, joy, and peace waiting for you, once you realize you can take authority over the dreadful memories of your past.

Just like the elephant, you already possess the power to break free from the strongholds of memories. Remember the saying, "Forgiveness doesn't set the offender free - it sets you free." Trust me, when it's all said and done, you will come to realize, the only prisoner is you.

Aren't you tired of waking up in the same emotional place you were yesterday, last week, last month, or last year? Seriously, are you tired? I was... and I decided I was no longer going to be hogtied and collared to past pains.

I finally tapped into the power that God had

already given me, and I broke the chains. I'm reminded of an old church song we use to sing, *I'm free, hallelujah I'm free, no longer bound, no more chains holding me, my soul is rested, it's such a blessing, thank God, hallelujah I'm free.* I'm free from the words my mom did or didn't say, I'm free from the painful heartache and heartbreak it caused.

I remember one day calling my mom and telling her that I loved her and there was nothing she could ever say or do to change that.

Of course, she was confused by my comment, but it's okay, I knew what I meant, and better yet, God knew. I wanted to be free and to this day my mom and I have a very healthy relationship, I love her dearly.

I also practice forgiveness with other people in my life. The supervisor, my neighbor, the rude cashier, the police, my Christian brothers and sisters, yep, they can do some damage, but that is manageable too.

The list can go on and on, but the word of God teaches us, there is nothing too hard for Him and that we can do all things through Christ who strengthens us. God's word says ALL THINGS, and all means all… it includes everything! It's a small word but it covers a lot of territory.

It is impossible to do it on your own, if we could, then it would not be the stronghold that it is. But guess what... you are not supposed to do it alone, you can't do it alone, so stop trying.

Stop treading water, struggling in the same place and not going anywhere. Go to your heavenly Father. Surrender the offense to God and tap into the power He has already given you, to set yourself free.

The captive elephant just moves back and forth, he's not going anywhere, he's moving yes, but he's not making any ground, he's not moving forward. Are you moving back and forth in the same place? Aren't you tired of dealing with the same thoughts, the same pain, and the memories of what happened?

Notice I used the past tense, HAPPENED? It's done, it's over, absolutely it was hurtful, offensive, and just plain wrong. But you can't change what happened to you in the past, you can only make a difference in your life going forward. Today is the day for you to be free!

Let's make ground today and move forward into the abundant life that was promised to all of us. The Lord has equipped you with all you need to break free and live a victorious life. Be freed from the strongholds of unforgiveness, you are more powerful than you think.

Luke 10:19

19 I have given you authority to trample on snakes and scorpions and to overcome all the power of the enemy; nothing will harm you.

Can you relate to the plight of the captive elephants?

# Forgive Of Course You Can

Forgive Of Course You Can

Forgive Of Course You Can

"It's better to forgive than to be tormented by unforgiveness."
– Angela Bowden

Forgive Of Course You Can

Chapter 7

Forgive and Be Free

This is a parable from the 18th chapter of Matthew, verses 23-35, where Jesus was teaching about forgiveness.

23 "Therefore, the kingdom of heaven is like a king who wanted to settle accounts with his servants. **24** As he began the settlement, a man who owed him ten thousand bags of gold was brought to him. **25** Since he was not able to pay, the master ordered that he and his wife and his children and all that he had be sold to repay the debt.

26 "At this the servant fell on his knees before him. 'Be patient with me,' he begged, 'and I will pay back everything.'

27 The servant's master took pity on him, canceled the debt and let him go."

28 "But when that servant went out, he found one of his fellow servants who owed him a hundred silver coins. He grabbed him and began to choke him. 'Pay back what you owe me!' he demanded."

29 "His fellow servant fell to his knees and begged him, 'Be patient with me, and I will pay it back.'"

30 "But he refused. Instead, he went off and had the man thrown into prison until he could pay the debt.

31 When the other servants saw what had happened, they were outraged and went and told their master everything that had happened."

32 "Then the master called the servant in. 'You wicked servant,' he said, 'I canceled all that debt of yours because you begged me to.

33 Shouldn't you have had mercy on your fellow servant just as I had on you?'

34 In anger his master handed him over to the jailers to be tortured, until he should pay back all he owed."

35 "This is how my heavenly Father will treat each of you unless you forgive your brother or sister from your heart."

Consider for a moment, who are you in this scenario? Are you the forgiving servant who had compassion and forgave the debt OR are you the selfish servant who withheld forgiveness even though he had been forgiven?

Verses 34 and 35 are so powerful and literally sums it up. God's word says we are to forgive our brothers and sisters from our heart! No exceptions.

The verses clearly state, the Lord will deliver you to the tormentors if you do not forgive, you will suffer, and you will be tormented.

Did you catch the part that said the servant would be tormented until all his debt was paid? Think about it, how long would it take for us to repay God for all the blessings and mercies he has bestowed upon us? He looked beyond our faults and saw our needs. I can't even begin to count the billion-plus *2nd chances* the Lord has given me.

The same God that extends you grace and mercy every day, forgives you for the things you do and say. He forgives you of all your wrongs. What gives you the right to withhold forgiveness and not pardon someone else?

You ask for forgiveness when you know you've done wrong, and God forgives you. So, I ask you again, who do you think you are?

Trust me, I had to come to this hard realization as well, I was stuck in this area for years. I was operating in disobedience and rebellion, but I wanted and needed change, I was tired. It was not easy to finally move forward and humble myself to God, but it became easier with time and practice.

My prayer for everyone reading this book, is that you become free. I pray that your journey to forgiveness is shorter than mine was. I pray you don't waste any more time, not one more second of your precious life, being chained to a memory.

I was truly tired of being sad. I wanted to be delivered, I wanted to move on and be free. I wanted the wall to come down, it was separating me from my mom and at the same time putting a strain on my other relationships. Finally, my desire to be free and love unconditionally had become bigger than the pain and bitterness inside of me.

When Jesus was betrayed, they lied about him, spit on him, mocked him, beat him with a whip, pressed a crown of thorns onto his head, nailed him to the cross, and then pierced his side. Jesus cried out, "Father forgive them for they don't know what they are doing." Can you imagine? After all that, he still asked the Father to forgive them. His love for us all out weighted the inhumane torture.

Surely none of us have ever experienced thorns being pressed into our heads, whips that snatch away pieces of our skins, or having a spear thrust into our sides. Jesus withstood all that and yet he still asked God to forgive the perpetrators. Again, I wonder who are we to withhold forgiveness?

YES, it's true that words can hurt. They can cut like a knife and live on forever, if you allow them to. BUT the love of God Never fails, it is forgiving and heals all wounds.

I know this to be true because the Love of Jesus forgave us, was literally nailed to the cross, died, and rose again, for you and me.

On this journey you will be faced with opposition and many offenses, you will need to be able to take the hit and keep moving. If you continually get stuck in your feelings, he can't trust you; the risk of you contaminating others with your offense and your pain, is too great.

Forgiveness is an act of surrendering, not to the person who hurt you, but to God. You're saying to Him; here I am, Lord have your way.

One thing's for sure, you can't go where the Lord wants to take you, in the condition you're in right now. Remember this, God will only change what you surrender to Him.

Ephesians 4:32

32 Be kind and compassionate to one another, forgiving each other, just as in Christ God forgave you.

Forgive Of Course You Can

Can you identify with these verses? Explain, it's good to speak and hear your own words.

Forgive Of Course You Can

Forgive Of Course You Can

Forgive Of Course You Can

"Time doesn't change things - you do."

– Angela Bowden

Forgive Of Course You Can

Chapter 8

Transformation

Since my house sits on a pond, I enjoy all types of wildlife. There are turtles, squirrels, snakes (yes snakes), blue birds, cardinals, hawks, egrets, you name it. I hear there are alligators in the area, but I haven't seen one yet, and I'm *really* okay with that.

I also have ducks in my backyard, seemingly generations of them. Sometimes they're even perched on the roof of my house which blows my mind. I love to sit on my patio, looking at the trees outlining the sky, it's the perfect place to start my day and enjoy nature.

I woke up one morning to a rainy wet day. However, the rain did not stop my morning routine. I got my coffee and headed to my patio for my prayer, praise, and devotion time.

As I began to wrap up my worship time, I looked up and I could see the dark clouds separating and the blue sky beginning to break through the darkness. It was clear that change was coming, and it was going to be a lovely day.

When I started my devotion time, there was

nothing but darkness all around me, it was raining, and things were looking very dreary. However, literally within minutes, the rain stopped, the clouds broke, and the blue skies came through, very boldly I might add, and it made me smile.

I realized as the sky began to get brighter and prettier, that this is exactly what forgiveness looks like. This is what freedom looks like. What started out as doom and gloom had taken on a whole new look, a new day, blue skies, and fresh air.

Just like the sky was transformed, through the spirit of forgiveness your life can open-up to more joy and peace within. You can see better, and you will feel a lot better. Nothing looks the same, nothing feels the same. You wake up with a smile, ready to experience whatever the day brings. You are literally free to be free.

I know some people say, when you forgive you forget, but that's not true at all. Unless something happens to your brain or your thought process, you will never forget what happened. However, when you've truly forgiven from your heart, the sting of the offense is gone, the memory remains.

It no longer makes you sad and holds you hostage because the power the offense had over you is gone. You have taken your power back; you have taken authority over the darkness that once consumed you. It can no longer produce emptiness and loneliness in your life... in your spirit.

Dr. Fred Luskin, of the Stanford University Forgiveness Project, describes forgiveness as, *"The feeling of peace that emerges as you take your hurt less personally, take responsibility for how you feel and become a hero instead of a victim in the story that you tell. Forgiveness is the experience of peacefulness in the present moment."*

Forgiving someone who has offended you, regardless of the offense, allows you to move on with your life, while trusting God's system of justice. No sin will go unnoticed. Free your mind to focus on loving God and living the life He wants for you. When you accept God's forgiveness, you'll be able to share with others.

We are all responsible for the relationships we're in. Whether it is with a sister, brother, friend, husband, wife, boyfriend, or girlfriend, both parties hold some responsibility for that relationship. That includes the good times and bad times, the mundane, and even the offenses.

Believe it or not, someone is watching you, they are taking notes on how you have responded to an offense. So, we must be aware of the impression we leave upon the people that are in our lives. They will learn positive AND negative behaviors from us. I don't know about you, but I would rather be a positive force in someone's life, as much as possible.

This is especially important if you have young children who are still in their formative years, because by the time they become teenagers, they have already learned from your example.

Do you want them to waste their precious living years focused on an offense? Do you want them to have the same horrible experiences you've had? Of course not, we all want our children to forgive others, move past the pains, and live a productive life. Now is the time to teach them what love and forgiveness looks like.

How do you want your children to impact this world? I hope with love. When I'm dead and gone, I want to leave a legacy of love and forgiveness for my children and for all who knew me.

NOW is the time for a change, time to set our sights higher, time to breathe again, time to think about all the things that bring you joy. There are quite a few wonderful things going on around you and for you... it's time to change direction and focus on those things.

This may sound a bit corny, but forgiveness will bring out the winner in you, and who doesn't want to win. I want to win at everything, I don't want anything to defeat me. We all know what winning feels like, right, so let's do it!

Revelation 21:1-4

Then I saw "a new heaven and a new earth," for the first heaven and the first earth had passed away, and there was no longer any sea. **2** I saw the Holy City, the new Jerusalem, coming down out of heaven from God, prepared as a bride beautifully dressed for her husband. **3** And I heard a loud voice from the throne saying, "Look! God's dwelling place is now among the people, and he will dwell with them. They will be his people, and God himself will be with them and be their God. **4** He will wipe every tear from their eyes. There will be no more death or mourning or crying or pain, for the old order of things has passed away."

Forgive Of Course You Can

Do you finally feel ready to move on? If so, what has changed?

Forgive Of Course You Can

Forgive Of Course You Can

Forgive Of Course You Can

> *"It still hurts because you're still holding on to it. Just let go."*
> *– Angela Bowden*

Forgive Of Course You Can

Chapter 9

The Awakening

Take a moment to envision your future, totally free of all the memories that stifled your life for days, months, or even years.

How beautiful is it to be able to visualize a better tomorrow, despite all that you've experienced, knowing that you no longer need to suffer through the pain of yesterday?

Whatever images you create in your mind can become a reality, just as sure as you can imagine it, you can attain it. That's why we must be careful about what we release into the atmosphere, because whatever you release, is what you will get back. Peace, love, and happiness; if these are the things you focus on, you will find they will manifest into reality, once you begin to sow the seed of forgiveness.

For the most part, we allow our emotions to take center stage. We must learn to take authority over our emotions and the desire to continue down the same path which leads to nowhere.

Determine in your soul that not one more day will pass where you struggle with letting go of the past.

Just let go. It's time for forward thinking. You need to begin to move forward, so you can master your emotions instead of them mastering you. It's time to take better care of yourself. A powerful remedy for self-care is forgiveness.

Free yourself. Keep in mind, when you truly forgive from the heart, you will no longer sit and wait for an apology that might never come. You will simply move on with your life. Until you free yourself, you are still tied, shackled, and tethered to your past pains. Give yourself this gift, don't EXPECT an apology.

If you continue to think the other person doesn't deserve forgiveness, then you *actually* place yourself in a position of needing forgiveness, funny how that works right!?!

Living your best life is way more productive than agonizing over an apology that may never come. I said it before and I'll say it again, maybe a lil differently... IT'S TIME TO GET ON WIT YO LIFE!!!!

There was a time when I was in a physically abusive marriage, I've been divorced now for over 30 years. I've moved on and I have completely forgiven my ex, but one day a few years ago God spoke to me about Him. I was driving in my car and I heard the Lord speak to me and say, *"Call him and let him know you forgive him."*

I thought, *NO, it's okay God, I don't need to call him, I forgave him a long time ago.* So, I didn't make the call, but the Holy Spirit would not leave me alone. For days the thought kept coming back to me and I continued to dismiss it. Then finally I realized, as a woman of God, I need to be obedient to the Holy Spirit.

I grudgingly picked up the phone, rolling my eyes in my head with every number I dialed. Even as the phone was ringing, I was still rolling my eyes as hard as I could, inhaling and exhaling as I did. Isn't it interesting how we behave when we think we know better than God?

When he answered the phone, I said hi, and I begin to tell him how the Lord had placed it on my heart to call. I told him that I had forgiven him for all the things he had done to me during our marriage.

To my surprise, as soon as I said those words, he started sobbing uncontrollably. He was so overcome with emotions I could not understand what he was saying. Once he had gathered himself, he thanked me, said he really needed to hear that, and how sorry he was. I told him he did not owe me anything, I just needed him to know he was forgiven.

I was floored, even though I had forgiven him long ago, I had no idea he needed to hear those words from me. Thank God, I was finally obedient and made the call - it felt like something had lifted off me. Forgiving and being forgiven is very liberating.

He has passed on now, which makes me even more thankful that he knew he was forgiven before he took his last breath.

I would like to share this poem that I found, written by Pat A. Fleming.

<u>Forgiveness Is Divine</u>

Some people view forgiveness,
As a virtue for the weak.
An act of Mercy undeserved,
That serves no useful need.

They stand firmly in their judgment,
And won't consider a mistake.
They prefer to hold a senseless grudge,
Then accept amends when made.

They feel they have some Godly right,
To reject and criticize.
They're possessed by righteous anger,
And consumed by pointless pride.

They're focused on how they've been wronged,
And won't be made the fool again.

So, they feel they must avenge themselves,
By refusing to give in.

They will sacrifice their family,
Or forsake a long-time friend.
Do anything they have to do,
To be the winner in the end.

Or perhaps it's that they can't resolve,
The depth of all their hurt.
Caused when someone that they've trusted,
Left them questioning their worth.

But no matter why the struggle,
Out of pride or out of fear.
Not being able to forgive,
Can cause the loss of ones most dear.

Yes, forgiveness is a virtue,
They even say it is divine.
But more than that it sets you free,
From what weighs you down inside.
The best way to approach this life,
Is to ask forgiveness and to forgive.
There's a balance to this crazy world,
So live and let live

2 Corinthians 5:17

17 Therefore, if anyone is in Christ, the new creation has come: The old has gone, the new is here!

Forgive Of Course You Can

What is the first thing you are going to do, to start the process?

Forgive Of Course You Can

Forgive Of Course You Can

Forgive Of Course You Can

"Forgiveness is a process don't waste any more time... set YOUR heart free." – Angela Bowden

Forgive Of Course You Can

Chapter 10

Triumphant

Well, here we are, at the end of our time together. I pray that your journey to forgiveness has begun and you do not give up until you reach freedom.

It is a wonderful place to find yourself, after spending so much time behind the bars of unforgiveness. It was indeed a journey and a very difficult one at that, however, I promise, you will see the fruit of your labor.

Just like you, I started from ground zero, feeling lost and hopeless. I wondered if I'd ever be able to move on with my life, believing I would never be able to put the past behind me. As I mentioned, I really didn't have a life of joy, I didn't have peace, and I felt very alone and isolated. But thank God, I got to a place where I realized I wasn't living the abundant life God had prepared for me.

I spent so much time in a valley of nothingness, until one day I decided I wanted to live, love, and feel loved. I knew the only way for me to get what I wanted was to have a heart transplant and higher forward thoughts.

I realized, unforgiveness had robbed me of many

years – but never again!

Let me be clear, as long as I live, I will have to deal with offense, because I don't live in a world of perfect people. However, the offense will not be able to take root in my spirit and I will NOT become entangled with unforgiveness. I will be affected of course, but not infected by it.

The sooner you realize you cannot control anyone but you... the better. I mean absolutely no control over anyone; how they feel, what they say, or what they don't say. Once you embrace that truth, your load will become a little bit lighter. When I understood and accepted that hard reality, it was my first step to the road of recovery and restoration.

On my journey to forgiveness, as I meditated and sought the Lord, I realized we must forgive in a way that honors God. We need to see people through the eyes of our Lord and forgive like He does.

God's word says, *blessed are the merciful, for they shall see mercy*. So, if we want mercy, we must show mercy.

The bible also teaches us that we reap what we sow, we must understand that whatever you put out into the universe, is what you will get back.

Like my grandfather used to say, "Good follow good, bad follow bad." As it relates to forgiveness, it is simple, don't expect to be forgiven if you are not forgiving.

Looking forward, I believe that you are in a different place now - a good place, and my prayer is that you come to experience how liberating forgiveness is.

Let's consider the cross. As Jesus was dying on that cross He said, "Father forgive them for they know not what they do." None of his accusers and torturers asked him for forgiveness, but He gave it to them anyway, because he knew they needed it. THAT'S LOVE!!! UNCONDITIONAL LOVE!!!

For me, forgiveness was a gift. I now have my family back. I love my mom, always have and always will, I NEVER STOPPED loving her. I'm completely healed from the past hurt and pain, I no longer feel isolated from the people that I love... my family and friends.

Twenty plus years ago the Lord placed it on my heart to write this book on forgiveness, I've done several messages or sermons on the subject.

Now I understand why the Lord kept this matter before me and so close to my heart. I know first-hand how destructive it can be and how tormented one can be when living in a perpetual state of unforgiveness.

Hebrew 12:1 tells us to lay aside every weight and the sin that so easily beset us. Not only is unforgiveness weighty, but it's also SIN. Now that we know better, it's high time we do better.

Remember we cannot afford to allow the enemy to have any sort of advantage over us... having that portal of unforgiveness open, gives the enemy an advantage over us.

Everything hinges on your ability to forgive. Your purpose, your destiny, your future, your relationships (all of them), your health, and your ministry, is riding on you being able to forgive.

You may still be thinking it's too hard, it's too much. Well you're right, it is too much, for YOU… but not for GOD. You'll never be able to do it on your own. That's why you must petition the Lord in prayer to help you. He brings restoration, mends your broken heart, and makes you whole again.

I've had to forgive a lot of people in the last few years and that's okay - I'm good with that. Even, and most importantly, when I feel like I haven't done anything wrong. It won't kill you, saying I'm sorry has never sent anyone into cardiac arrest.

For the sake of peace, and for me to move forward, this approach works for me. Which speaks to my spiritual growth.

As I look back over my life and where the Lord has brought me from, I'm amazed at the journey AND how much better I've become at forgiving others. *I'm sorry* is two of the most healing words you will ever come to know.

So, I encourage you to seek the awesome freedom that forgiveness in Christ can provide and to give that freedom to someone else TODAY.

Matthew 6:9-12

9 This, then, is how you should pray: "'Our Father in heaven, hallowed be your name,

10 your kingdom come, your will be done, on earth as it is in heaven.

11 Give us today our daily bread.

12 And forgive us our debts, as we also have forgiven our debtors.

Forgive Of Course You Can

How does it feel to be walking toward your freedom?

Forgive Of Course You Can

About the Author

Angela realized at a very early age that she had a heart for the people of God. As a little girl, not even understanding why, friends and relatives would come to her asking for prayer, requesting that she lay hands on them.

Angela's parents maintained a home full of Christian values throughout her youth, which carried through to her adult life. It is the same Christian foundation on which she stands today.

Throughout her journey as a follower of Christ, Angela served as a leader in a variety of ministries. She led in Women's Ministry, the Benevolent Ministry, the Usher Board Ministry, and the New Member Orientation, while serving and assisting in other ministries as needed. In August 2007, she became an Ordained Minister.

Every Sunday, after church service, Angela served as a volunteer in the ICU at St. Joseph Hospital, which opened the door for her to start a Sunday Ministry, visiting the sick and their families in their time of crisis. She was also instrumental in what some would call a *street ministry*, where she initiated an evangelizing ministry in the housing community of Belmont Heights.

Through all her years of ministry, God used Angela to encourage and bring hope to those around her, even as she struggled with her own challenges of unforgiveness. However, through prayer and the re-positioning of her heart, she is now free!

Angela invites you to contact her to share your story and journey to forgiveness.

ForgiveOfCourseYouCan@Gmail.com

Angela Bowden
P.O. Box 22524
Tampa, FL 33630

Follow Angela on Facebook and Instagram!

Facebook.com/ForgiveOfCourseYouCan

Instagram.com/ForgiveOfCourseYouCan

Bibliography

Scripture quotations and references are all taken from the Holy Bible, (NIV) New International Version.

The poem, Forgiveness is Divine, was authored by Pat A. Fleming and published online at familyfriendpoems.com/poem/forgiveness-is-divine.

Excerpts from "Forgiveness: An Antidote for Healing of the Body, Mind, Soul and Spirit," authored by Reverend Yvonne McCoy, Retired Chaplain, from Morton Women's and Children's Hospital. Norton Church and Health Ministries published it in their October 10, 2014 newsletter.

Sheryl Walters published the article in Natural News, (May 26, 2008) citing the work of Dr. Frederic Luskin of Stanford University and Director of the Stanford Forgiveness Project.

Forgive Of Course You Can

www.ingramcontent.com/pod-product-compliance
Lightning Source LLC
LaVergne TN
LVHW052254070426
835507LV00035B/2840